Easy Piano

Disney
Christopher Robin

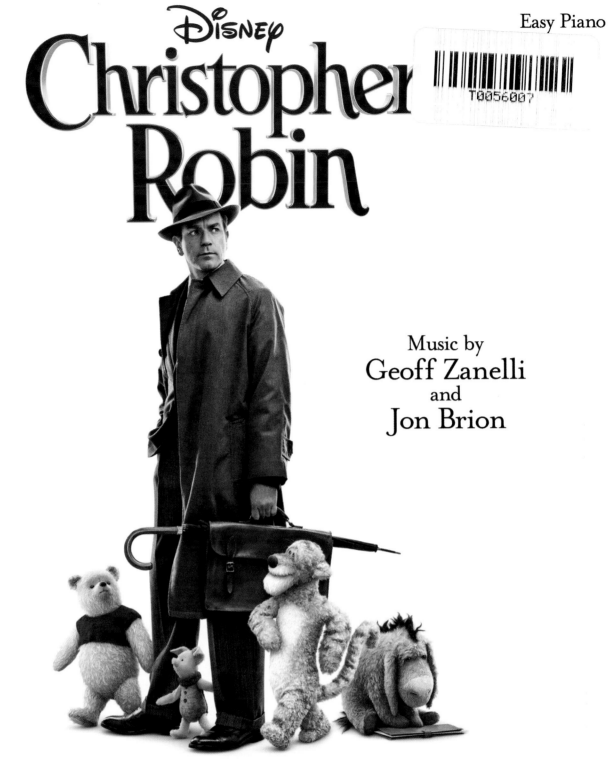

Music by
Geoff Zanelli
and
Jon Brion

Music from the Motion Picture Soundtrack

Disney Characters and Artwork TM & © 2018 Disney

Based on the "Winnie the Pooh" works by A.A. Milne and E.H. Shepard.

ISBN 978-1-5400-3872-2

Visit Hal Leonard Online at
www.halleonard.com

Contact Us:
Hal Leonard
7777 West Bluemound Road
Milwaukee, WI 53213
Email: info@halleonard.com

In Europe contact:
Hal Leonard Europe Limited
Distribution Centre, Newmarket Road
Bury St Edmunds, Suffolk, IP33 3YB
Email: info@halleonardeurope.com

In Australia contact:
Hal Leonard Australia Pty. Ltd.
4 Lentara Court
Cheltenham, Victoria, 3192 Australia
Email: info@halleonard.com.au

Contents

STORYBOOK

Music by GEOFF ZANELLI

Moderately

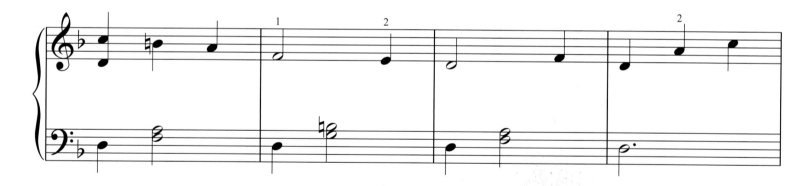

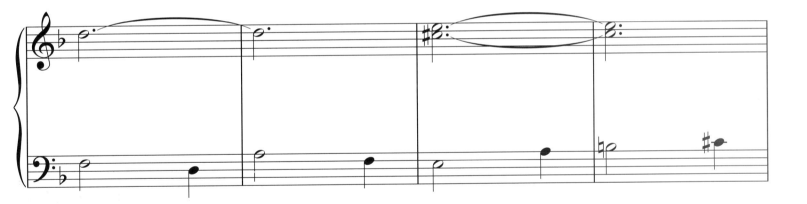

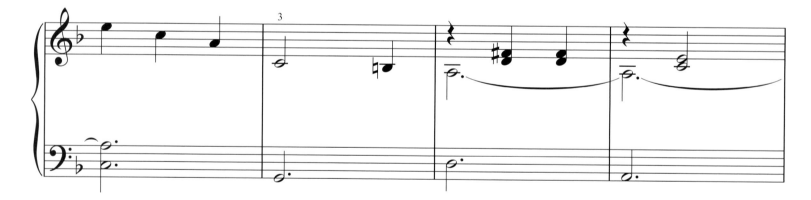

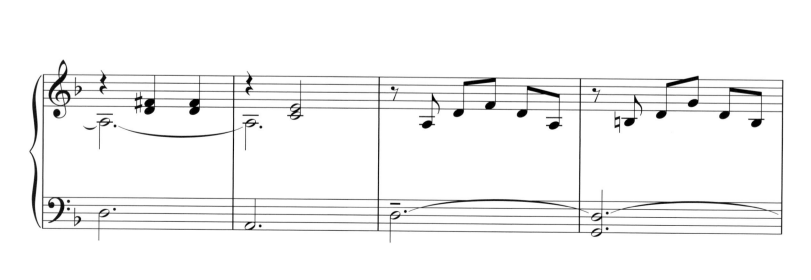

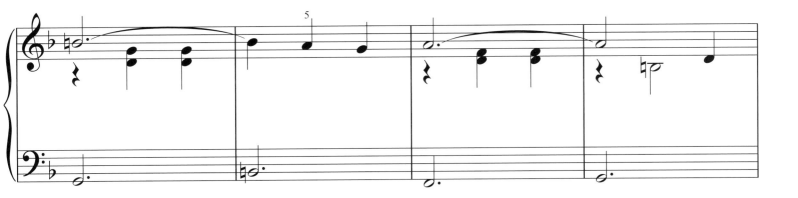

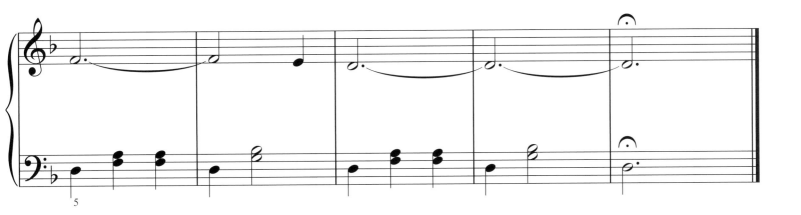

NOT DOING NOTHING ANYMORE

Music by JON BRION

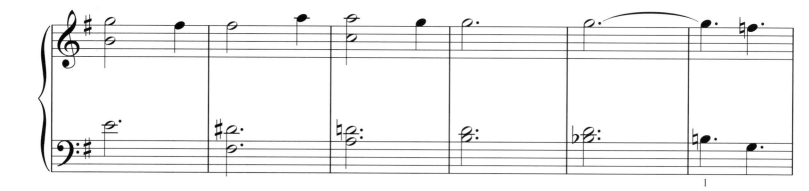

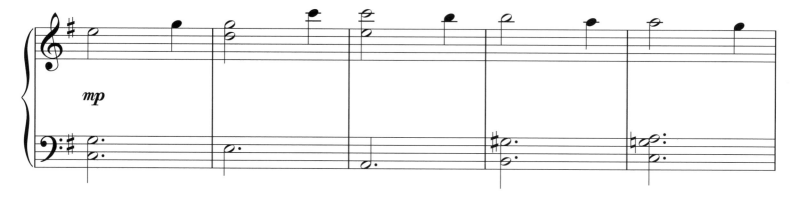

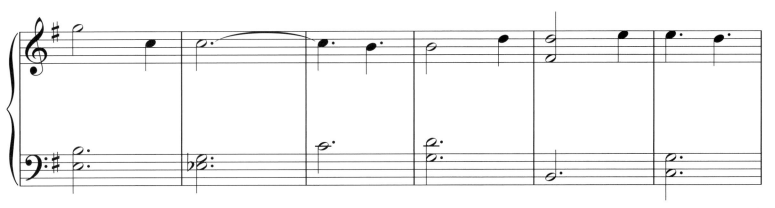

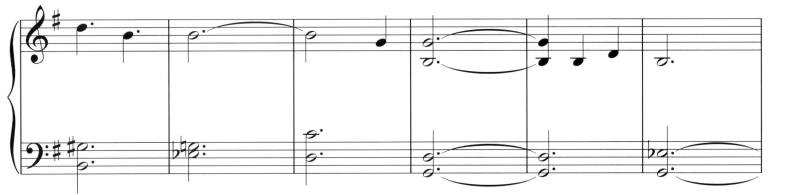

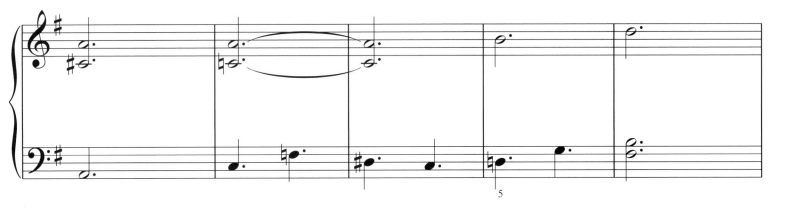

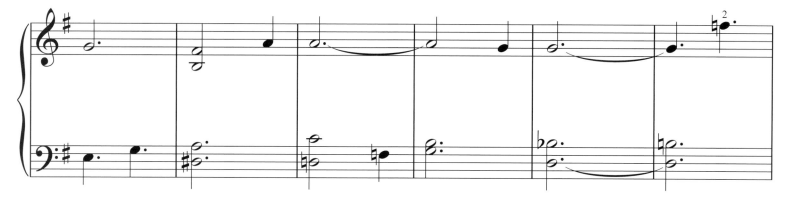

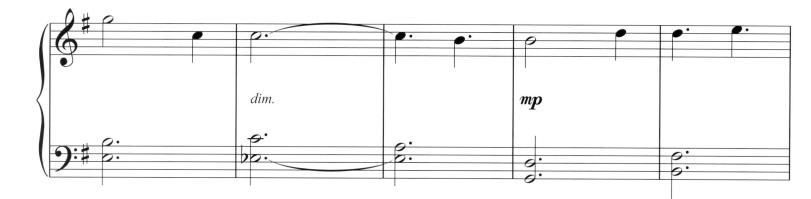

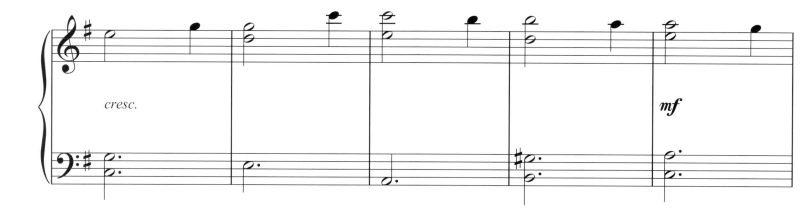

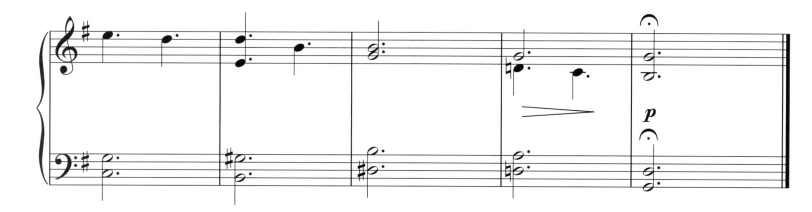

GOODBYE, FAREWELL

Music and Lyrics by
RICHARD M. SHERMAN

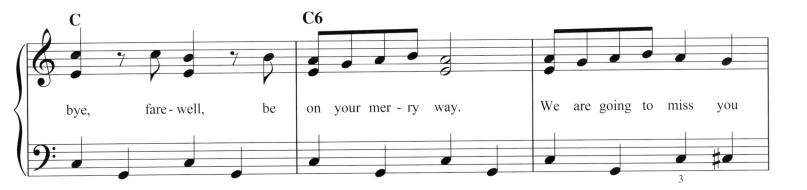

taa and too - dle - oo.　On my mer - ry way I'll　al - ways think of you.　On

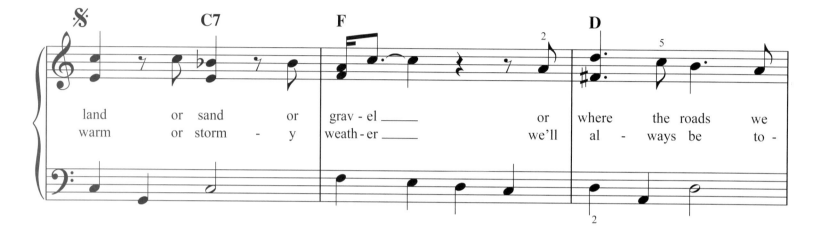

land　or sand　or　grav - el ____　or　where　the roads　we
warm　or storm - y　weath - er ____　we'll　al - ways be　to -

trav - el　un - rav - el. It's more　fun　with two,　it's　al - ways me and you　and to -
geth - er　for - ev - er. For with -　in　my heart,　if　we should ev - er part, we'll be

To Coda ⊕

geth - er　we will　stay.　Dum,　dum,　di, dum,　di,
nev - er　far a -

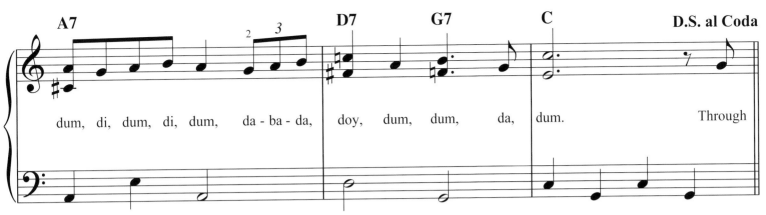

EVELYN GOES IT ALONE

Music by GEOFF ZANELLI

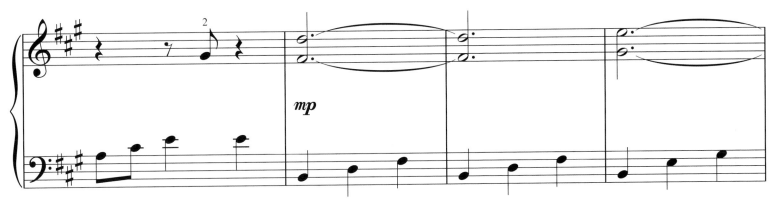

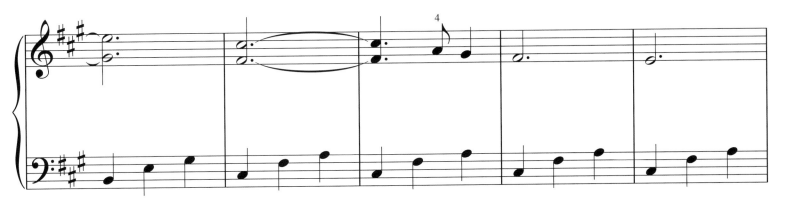

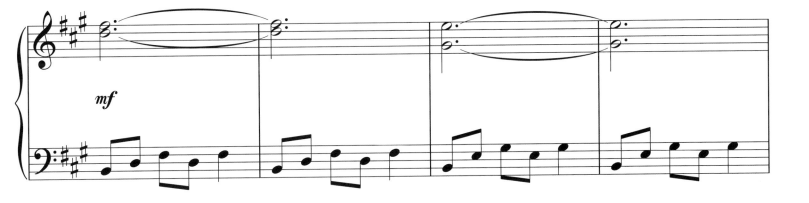

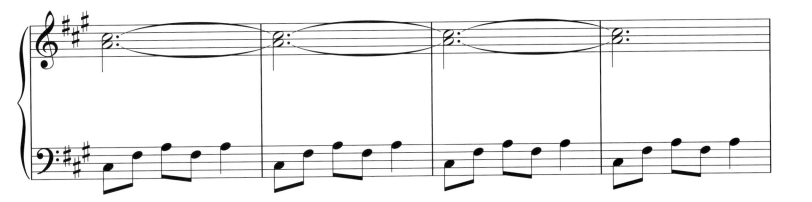

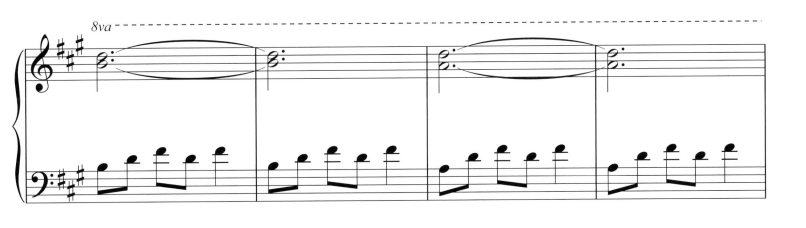

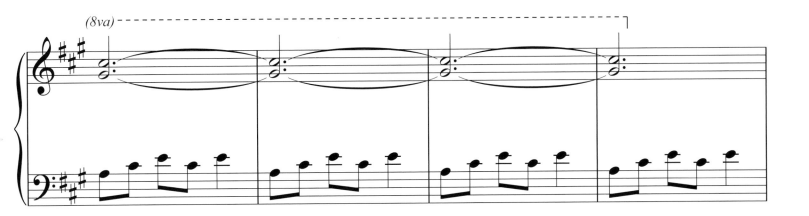

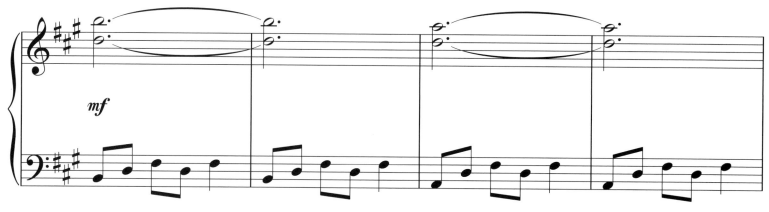

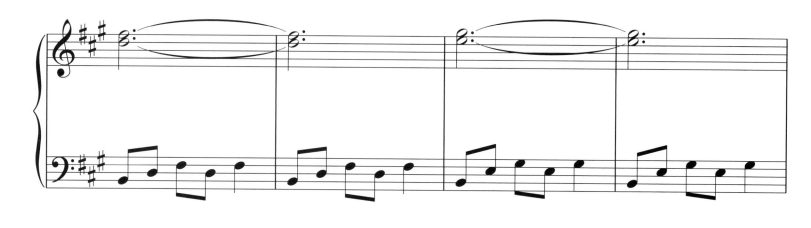

THROUGH THE TREE

Music by GEOFF ZANELLI

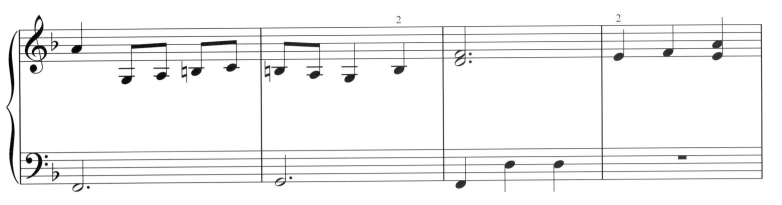

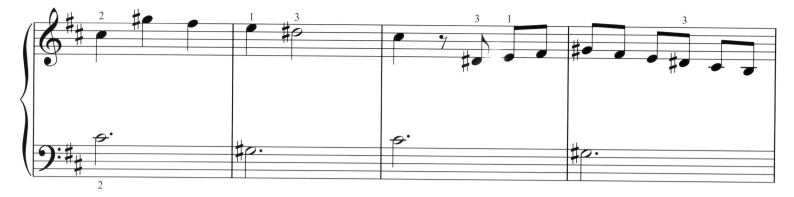

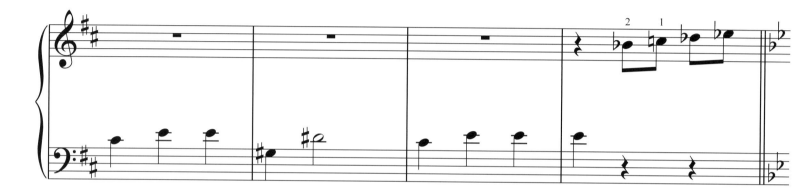

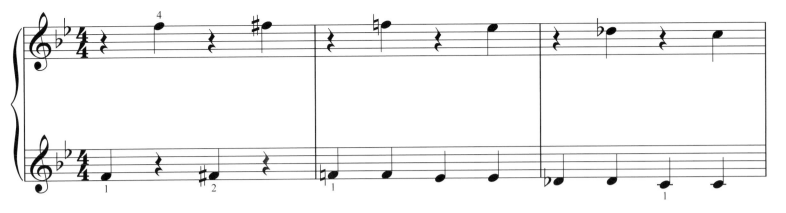

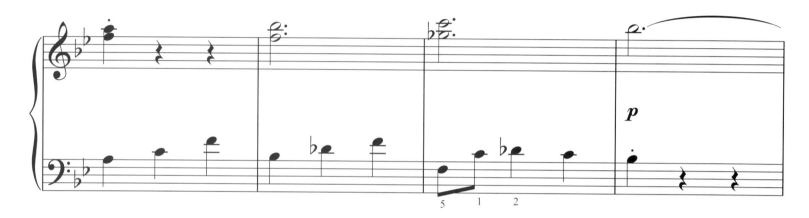

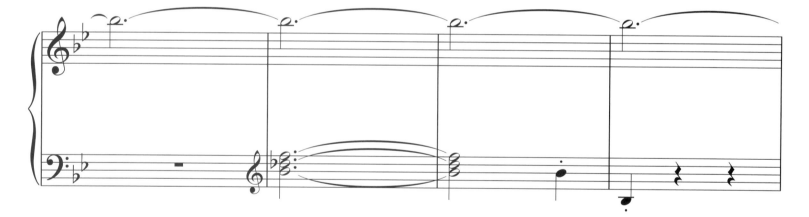

MY FAVORITE DAY

Music by GEOFF ZANELLI
and JON BRION

Slowly

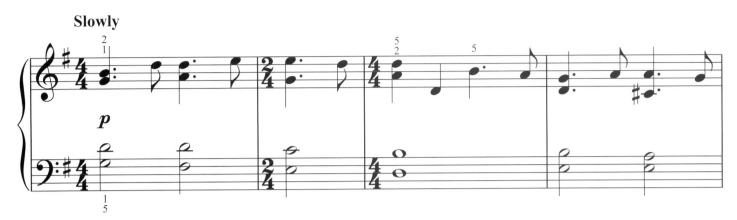

With more motion

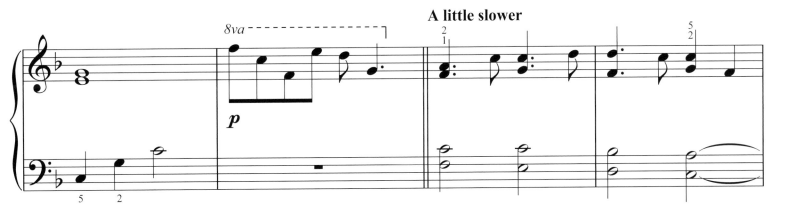

A little slower

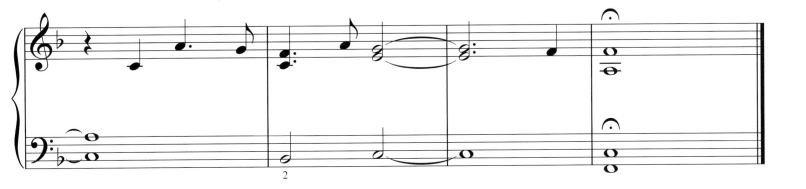

HEFFALUMP BATTLE

Music by JON BRION

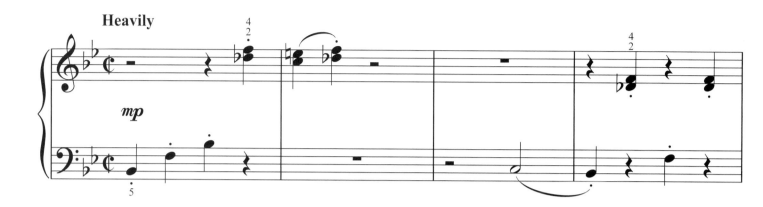

Much slower

Quickly

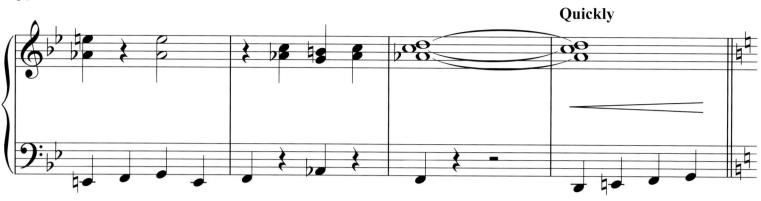

Much slower

BUSY DOING NOTHING

Music and Lyrics by
RICHARD M. SHERMAN

Moderately, with a bounce

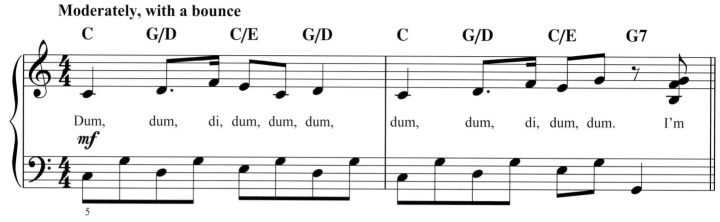

Dum, dum, di, dum, dum, dum, dum, dum, di, dum, dum. I'm

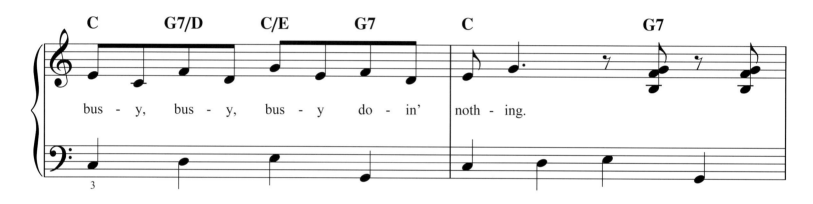

bus - y, bus - y, bus - y do - in' noth - ing.

Do - ing noth - ing, that's the life for me. For

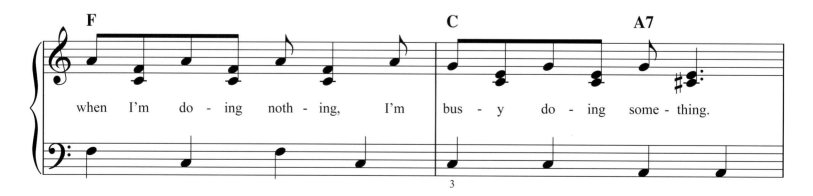

when I'm do - ing noth - ing, I'm bus - y do - ing some - thing.

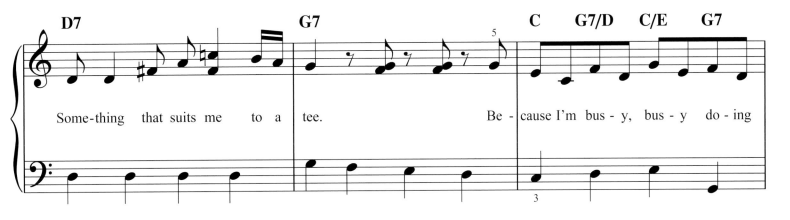

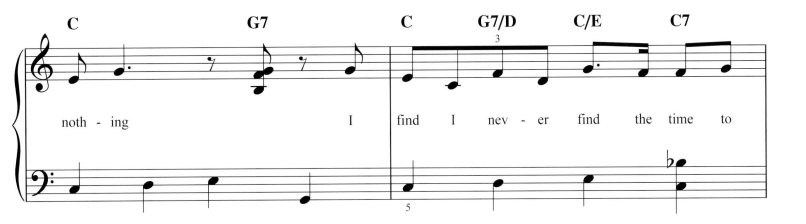

CHRISTOPHER ROBIN

Music and Lyrics by
RICHARD M. SHERMAN

Moderately, with freedom

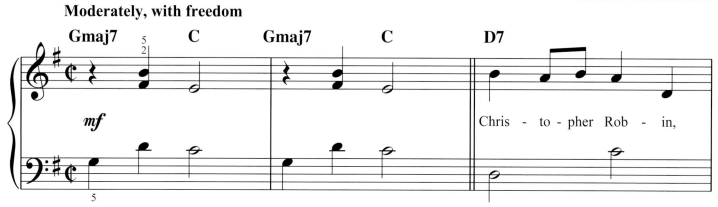

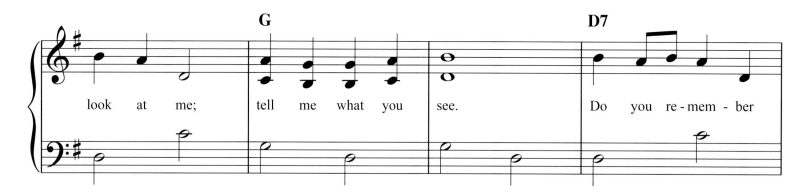

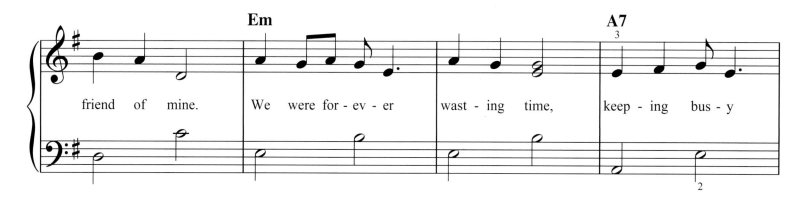

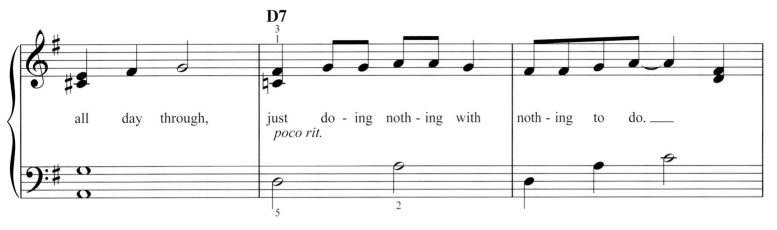

all day through, just do-ing noth-ing with noth-ing to do.___

poco rit.

Gath-er-ing a-corns off the ground;_ pick-ing up Pooh sticks

a tempo

all a-round;_ dream-ing of some-thing not to do; just be-ing us, be-ing

poco rit.

me and you. Chris-to-pher Rob-in, can't you see? From the ver - y

a tempo

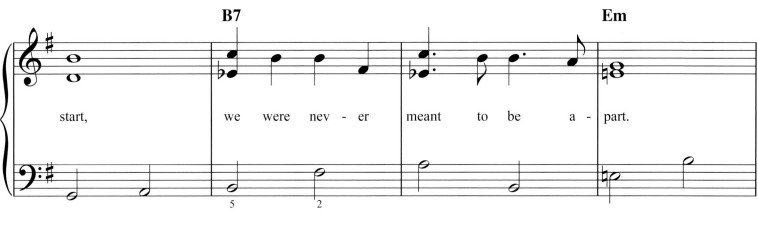

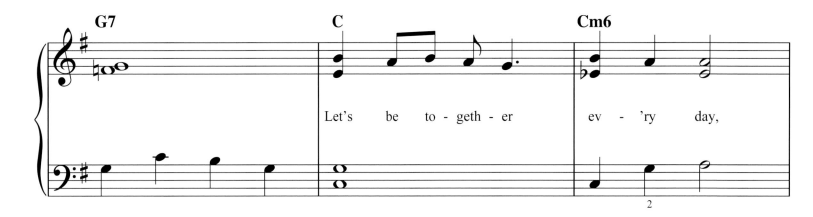

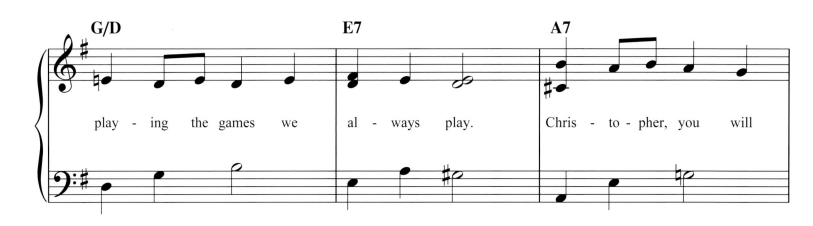

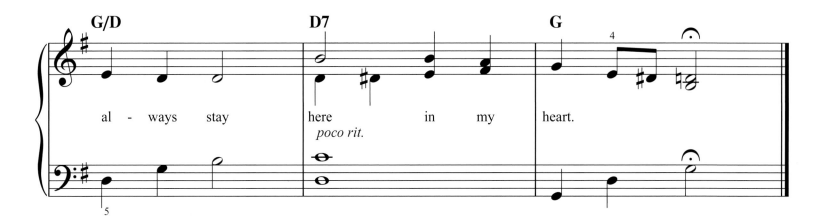